LIFE'S BEAUTIFUL GAME

RHYTHMICAL MIKE

Best wishes!
Thank you so much!!

Although the author and publisher have made every effort to ensure that the information in this book was correct at press time, the author and publisher do not assume and hereby disclaim any liability to any party for any loss, damage, or disruption caused by errors or omissions, whether such errors or omissions result from negligence, accident, or any other cause.

Production 2018
Lavender and White Publishing,
Galway,
Ireland.
Email info@lavenderandwhite.co.uk

© MIKEY MARKHAM 2018

The moral right of the author has been asserted

Typesetting, layout and design Lavender and White Publishing

www.lavenderandwhite.co.uk

Rhythmical Mike is a spoken word artist from Derbyshire. He performs across the UK and has made recent appearances in venues as diverse as YNot festival, Bearded theory, London's Chill Pill, Sheffield Hallam University, sharing the stage with high profile artists such as Russell Brand, Rizzle Kicks, Hollie McNish and Akala.

As well as poetry performances, Rhythmical Mike regularly runs poetry workshops and recitals for schools, youth centres, charities and more around the country. He spoke at the Telegraph Festival of Education 2017. Rhythmical Mike's poetry will be featured in a forthcoming publication from Independent Thinking Press, 'Working Class' edited by Ian Gilbert. His first collection of poetry is soon to be published "Life's beautiful game".

Rhythmical Mike is also a star of YouTube, with poems such as 'Smile' and 'You Got This' gaining many thousands of hits. His short film of 'Life's Beautiful Game' is winning him admirers across the world.

Heartfelt and honest, Rhythmical Mike's poetry has a profound ability to inspire and motivate all those who have the chance to listen to his words…

Martin Illingworth, Sheffield Hallam University

Mikey is the living embodiment of the adage to 'speak quietly but carry a large stick'. With a quiet resolution, he cleverly puts into soft words strong stories of love, life and death to create spoken-word poetry with which he assaults the heart of his mesmerised audience.

Ian Gilbert, award-winning author and editor

Acknowledgements:

I'd like to thank my loving, supportive and patient family. I'm sure the day I told you I was going to make a living as a poet, it didn't sit too well at first. Without you none of this would have been possible. Martin Illingworth for the flattering foreword, taking me into different classroom environments, pushing me out of my comfort zone, constant words of wisdom and being a genuine true friend. You don't realise how much you have inspired me. Ian Gilbert from Independent Thinking for asking me to be a part of the ITL family. It's an honour to be associated with such characters.

To everyone who has provided a platform for me to perform on: Thank you to Adam Illingworth for the book cover graphic design and Francis Jagger for the image, Dan Webber- furthest from the sea(my first gig), Miggy Angel(speech therapy), Leon Poetry(Howl), Joe WordLife Kriss(WordLife), Matt Abbott, Toria Garbutt, Louise Fazackerley (Nymphs + thugs), Toby Campion, Jess Green (find the right words), Will Horspool aka PoetMan, Gemma Baker and Leanne Moden.

Sophie Sparham and Jamie Thrasivoulou – the word wise team who continue to achieve and inspire.

To all my friends in the music and poetry scene for your love, listening and care; Lewis Brade, Nick McCann, Mollie Hughes, Alex young, Dathan Horridge, Luke Jagger, Oliver Cowlishaw, Hywel Roberts, Trevor Wright, Pr@xis, Cullen Marshall, Johnny Swinhoe, Pippa Nayer, Gaz Peacham, Kane Ashmore, Robyn Johnson, Dean atta, Zack Purdy, Kirst Taylor, Charlie Juster, Jake Farell, Darren Blair.

To you the reader – keeping the arts and creative scene alive.

Peace, love, compassion, altruism, kindness and all that jazz.

Rhythmcial Mike

Foreword

Some people just have to **make** their own way in life because the message they receive from society at large about their value throws them off the path that they might well have chosen for themselves. This is no easy thing.

If you are being told that something is out of your reach, then you are likely to stop reaching. You might not even notice that the thing that really creates **your spark** is even there. We are impressionable beings; we need affirmation, we need someone to notice and we need someone to tell us that we have a special talent for something; and that, that special talent is of interest.

Imagine being told that you can't write, that you can't explain how the world looks... but there is something inside you that tells you the opposite. We need to listen to that 'can do' voice more often. Those that can block out the doubters and listen to their instincts, and their dreams, without faltering, are a rare breed. And those that can overcome this injustice without malice are fewer still.

Mikey Markham has a profound impact on those that have the good fortune to hear his spoken word performances. Now that good fortune spreads to the printed page.

Let us meet with a smile
For the smile is the beginning of love I've found

Mikey is one of those old souls that **know** about this life. He possesses the wisdom of ages without the inconvenience of actually being old. His poetry is confessional, autobiographical and honest but it invites us all to consider how we feel about our own worlds. His themes are universal; Mikey wants you to celebrate **being alive** and to think about how to make best use of the time you might have been allocated.

I have had the opportunity to see first-hand the way that Mikey's poetry can delight and provoke, gladden and sadden, soothe and irk - his words are a sensory workout for the heart and head. Mikey would like to share with you, discuss with you, listen to you and get to know your story; I commend him and his words to you.

Martin Illingworth - Sheffield, November 2017

Quotes/Comments

There are very few in this world who turn rhythm, rhyme & the art of creative lyrics into powerful emotive words that hit your soul. Rhythmical Mike's magic with the spoken word will leave you speechless and in awe of his craft. He's a rare artist indeed.

Nina Jackson @musicmind

Rhythmical Mike takes the spoken word and elevates it to an art form that demands our attention. His ability to take us through the peaks and troughs of modern life with his pin sharp utterances and hypnotic rhythms enables all of us to reflect, refresh and renew our own thoughts and actions.
Simply put, he is the very definition of 'Poetry in motion'!!

Dave Keeling

Rhythmical Mike is more than an expert observer of day to day frailties. He is more than a highly skilled wordsmith line-dancing with linguistics. He is a carrier of meaning. A tour-de-force of gentle understanding. He needs to be heard because he listens so well.

Hywel Roberts

Mikey is the living embodiment of the adage to 'speak quietly but carry a large stick'. With a quiet resolution, he cleverly puts into soft words strong stories of love, life and death to create spoken-word poetry with which he assaults the heart of his mesmerised audience.

Ian Gilbert, award-winning author and editor

Heartfelt and honest, Rhythmical Mike's poetry has a profound ability to inspire and motivate all those who have the chance to listen to his words…

Martin Illingworth, Sheffield Hallam University

"If I feel physically as if the top of my head were taken off, I know that is poetry. These are the only ways I know it. Is there any other way?"

Emily Dickinson

Engaging. Creative. Powerful. Heartfelt.
With every word Rhythmical Mike demonstrates his deep understanding, his compassion and his gentle determination to influence change for our young people.
His power of the spoken word demands to be listened to.

Katy Hodges

To all the artists involved… Thank you so much! Your contributions are invaluable. It truly is an honour to have such talented friends.

Illustrations:

CHANGE - Guy Roberts (Thunk Visual)

TRICKSTER – Kennedy Jo Noon

IS IMMAGRATION KILLING THE NATION? –Megan Allen (Facebook - Very Vegan Megan - Insagram – Veryveganmegan_art)

CLASS EDUCATION – Emily Alys King (Instagram – emilyartsandcrafts)

SHOOT TO KILL – Guy Roberts (Thunk Visual)

DOMESTIC SILENCE- Anna Marshall (Instagram – afredamarshall)

LOST- AJ Hazeldene

WHAT IS BEAUTY AT SCHOOL? Cai Antoney

"PLAY"GROUND- Sasha Palmer

LIKE YOU- Cai Antoney

MANS BEST FRIEND- Frances Jagger (Francesjaggercreates)

TROLL – Lucy Monaghan (Instagram - Unproductive_mermaid)

5 NATURAL EMOTIONS – Velma Brocklesby

NEWS – Eve Morris

SMILE–Nansy Ferret-Campbell (Facebook–NansyFerrettCampbell – Twitter - @Monster_Nip)

THIS IS ALLWE'VE GOT (PART 2) – Jade Gilmore

WHEN WE MEET AGAIN – Robyn Wallis Johnson (instagram-

Contents

CHANGE

It can happen you know

You don't have to feel
this lost sensation
You can become real,
No more sleeping around
Losing your soul,
Using the beer to fill in the hole,
Working every hour of each day
Clutching on to your next bit of pay,
Are those new shoes working for you?
Or has the anaesthetic work off like old glue?
That new Nike top
Or

Adidas hat,
Has the pain gone away?
Or are emotions still flat?
Does the idea of revaluation sound crazy?
Or are we just feeling helpless and lazy?
In order to think that a change is not needed,
You must somehow feel the systems succeeded,
Why are we accepting selfish acts?
Of governments stealing and ignoring the facts,
It can happen you know
A change can come,
Let's get a connection and all become one,
The dead human ape has fulfilled its role
Let's push much further and elevate the soul,
Our planet is dying
Politicians are lying
Please don't sit there with mindless complying,
If you're feeling lost
Or you're feeling alone
Don't think the answers are completely unknown,
The answers are here
They are from within,
Don't feel unwanted
Just step right in.

TRICKSTER

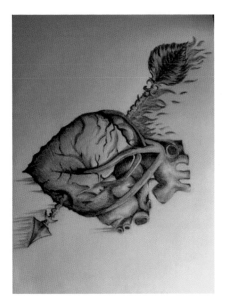

Nightmarish Paralysis
Sleepless nights

I'm trapped in you

boxed in   suffocated

With no vision and   no mind,

I'm stuck in you
Glued to a blank canvas and feel I'm going blind,

You're hard faced like concrete and can be as cold as ice,
You make my heart miss a beat and don't think twice,
You tempt me in   then throw me away and remind me I can't go
without you,

Every time you pull me back in I never want to have to doubt you,
But I do,
Because I know in you,
There's a lot of
Fire   anger   and pain,
I've felt the sunshine
But I've really
REALLY felt the rain,

Within the gods you're a trickster   a bow and arrow amongst
men
You draw   you aim   you shoot
And hit bulls eye
Again and again and again

You're in every book, film, music, art piece
Pretty much everywhere I seem to go,
So why am I so god damn scared of you?
That's one question I feel I'm never going to know,
BUT LOVE
Whoever you are?
Whatever you are?
Wherever you are?

THANK YOU

Because I couldn't live without you.

SPOKEN WORD

I genuinely believe spoken word can change your life

And the world

Here's how
Now,
STEP 1:- PICK UP A PEN
Then count to 10
Breathe
Don't need to tense your fingers to your palm,
Stay calm,
STEP 2:- this is all about you
I want to hear your story I promise it won't bore me,
The only thing you have that is unique
IS YOU

Use this that's all you can do,
There's an infinite platform no limitations of what you can say
Just find your style
Do it your way,
You can talk
ReallyReallyReally fast
Or
V e r y   p r e c i s e   a n d   s l o w,
You're the creator
You're in control
You get to pick your flow,
Write what you're feeling
Maybe something concealing
It might be revealing
But boy it's healing,
What's in your head
Allow it to be said,
You can
But don't need metaphor
To get inside your mind soul explore,
STEP 3:- What are you trying to tell me?
What message are you trying to display?
Have you walked your path?
Done it your way?
It can be
Deep and dark,
Passion and spark,
Humorous and light,
With wisdom and sight,
Narrative story,
Graphic and gory,
GET ANGRY AND MAD,
Or
Just tell me the tales you've had,

Know your intentions
Who's the audience?
What's the piece for?
If the writing's honest
They're going to want more,
STEP 4:-this is the unwritten spoken word universal law
Are you sure,
This piece of art is where your heart lies?
What's the real you?
You don't need a disguise
You're portraying the stories that have entered your eyes,
Do it for yourself
To be wise wins the prize,
STEP 5:- TAKE THE DIVE,
Art's about continually jumping off of cliffs
And developing your wings on the way down,
Don't worry too much about grammar
I'm still learning the difference from a verb and a noun,
To live a creative life
You must lose the fear of being wrong,
If your art's from the heart,
It's the best place to start,
And your content will always be strong,
The worst enemy to creativity has always been self-doubt,
If the verse feels right,
And the rhyme feels tight,
There's absolutely no need to back out,
Allow yourself to make mistakes
Know which ones to keep,
You never have to censor yourself,
You never have to change a
S~~#~#~###!T
To a
Bleeeeeeeeeeeeeep

Have a wild mind
But a disciplined eye,
Mind like the sky,
But scope of a spy,
STEP 6   STEP 7   STEP 8   STEP 9
This is the time to perfect your rhyme,
Repeat   Repeat   Repeat
Let your mouth run like an athlete,
To a beat,
Down the street,
Whoever you meet,
On your own,
Down the phone,
Fall in love with your material
Don't leave it alone,
Treat it as your first born
Or
As your best friend,
When you start reading don't be rushing for the end,
Believe in and
Mean every single word you have wrote,
Take pride in spoken word
It's time to take note,

O YEAH!

STEP 10:- Do it all over again
And follow NO RULES
Including mine,
Use this advice
You'll do just fine,
The ink
Your words
More powerful than knives,

Discover yourselves
Better your lives,
I hope it does for you what it's done for me,
Liberate your soul
Set yourself
free…

IS IMMIGRATION KILLING THE NATION

The way I see it is...

We live on a rock hurtling through infinite space,
So why are we making this piece of land such an uncomfortable place,
Where you can easily be judged by the colour of your face,

If we
Get into a rocket
And go to the moon
Look at the world like a
Big balloon what would
You see? You'd see
Water and land
So how can
We tell

P
E
O
P
L
E

Where they can and can't stand?

There are no invisible lines   dividing us all,
So can we please stop making the powerless

Feel so small,
We've all literally won the lottery just being here,
Do you really want to live that in constant fear?
Anger
Irritability
Division,
Because that's down to you
And that's your decision!

It takes so much effort to HATE another being.
So just change your mind-set
Change what you're seeing
If
You see somebody different to you
Near your family home
Don't let your mind be hit with hatefully roam,
Understand that's just another person there,
That feels your exact same emotions and can feel your stare,
If you look in his eyes and feel his soul,
Understand that
Happiness and surviving is his only goal,

Our
G
e
n
e
t
i
c
Material
Is practically the same,
So please don't let living be such a painful game,

"Them dirty immigrants and benefit cheats,"
"Completely fucking up all of our streets,"
But!
Here are some facts I'd like you to see,
Who is the real problem?
Who could it be?

Benefit cheats costing: 3.4 billion

Tax evasion: 70 billion

So this deep inner anger you're told to feel,
Directed at immigrants who want their lives to become real,
Might not be the reason society has fallen,
It seems that the higher powers are the people we should be calling,

So picture this

YOU
Were born in a worn torn township
From the wrong roll of life's dice,
And your only nutrition is chewing on some 3-day old rice,
Wouldn't you have very strong urges

To get away from a place where death daily emerges?
And you're told of a life of
Living
Wonder
And opportunity
Well
I say come join us
Come join our community

CLASS EDUCATION

Wake up at 5:45…
"This is a lie in …it feels like a gift,"
Dad's long gone for work
Mum should just about be finishing her shift,
Make my way down stairs trip over piled up newsletters, flyers, old post,
I serve my little sister milk, jam and burnt toast,
Rummage round the house like a dog chasing a scent,
"I've lost my bloody books and bag again,"
                    "O no …"
"Today is the assignment',…."
"Ahhhhhhh thank god for that"
"But how did they end up at the back of the T.V.?"
"Don't worry about it"
"Gotta run"
Look at the clock

It's 7:50,...
Brush my teeth like a nutter
Glance down and see spilt Toothpaste on my top...
"shit I've got rips in my shoes,"
"This isn't the life that I'd ever choose,"
"gotta move fast though, can't be late"
"I've been threatened... well warned this is 'the' last time,"
Why are they treating me like I've committed some kinda crime?

Missed the bus...
Pegged it to school in showering rain arrive at just past 9,
"Phew"
It's a substitute today, so I should be fine...
First lesson
ENGLISH
"Great this should be fun,"
"I wish this day was over but it's only just begun,"
Sit down and asked to read in 15 minute silence out of a ripped up old book,
8 lines in and I'm already stuck,
excogitate. magnanimous. opsimath
"Is anyone going to help me out here?"
The silence is unbearable
I pray they don't ask me a question as I just sit in constant fear,
"I mean"
"We've got about 2 bloody books in our house"
"When it comes to reading I ain't too keen,
"O... unless we are including Mum's Heat magazines,"
But I'm not too fussed about them either
"I don't want to know what Kim and Kanye do with their money,"
"Because we've bloody got none and I'm not trying to be funny,"
I grin and bear the rest of the lesson but feel lost and alone,
This is the moment reality kicks in
Knowing I'm going to be stuck in some grey old call centre answering the phone...

The day rolls on...
The lessons continue in the exact same routine,
Sit...
Listen intently...
"Repeat after me..."
"Feels we're part of a machine..."
Where some do well and some excel because they can regurgitate information,
Don't ask questions and DO NOT stand out...
Be upright...
In a certain formation,
I walk around the school yard as the day goes by Imagining being in the FA Cup playoff,
What really excites me is sport, music and art but everyone reminds me that it will never pay off,
Luckily art's the last lesson of the day
But not feeling great,
I've barely ate so finding it hard to concentrate,
The end of the lesson I pick up my bag and stumble towards the door,
But Miss Robison could feel something wasn't quite right and she wasn't prepared to ignore it,
"James!"
"Before you go can you just come here for a minute?"
"I turn around and demand "WHY!?"
Look hollow... downhearted ... deflated... as I wipe a tear out of my eye,
"Tell me what's troubling you James,"
"I can see you're not happy let's try and sort things out,"

"There's nothing you can do"
"I'm trapped in this prison"
"I'm never going to break out,"
"Every day I turn up like an obedient little animal and just sit clueless in the back of the room trying to keep my head down,

"It's either that or I have to try and gain attention by acting part of the class clown,"
"I've been labelled dyslexic...autistic...dyspraxic...BIG idiot with ADHD,"
"Got absolutely no idea what's truly wrong with me,"

Miss Robinson
Looks me in the eyes,
Gives me a warm smile and opens up her heart,
"Listen James"
"Where do I start?"
"My Dad always use to say to me"
"'If you judge a fish on its ability to climb it will go through its life thinking it's dumb,"
"Don't write yourself off so quick as your journey has just begun,"
"Don't worry about moulding or becoming a certain shape and size,"
"You do you... that's all you can do...that splits the clever from the wise,"
Don't let the system take control separate and divide,
Stick to your strengths... Stick to your passions purse them with love and pride,
This is your future
"This is your reality!"
"Make it as exciting as you want it to be,"
"The moment you realise you're an individual is the moment you'll be set free."

SHOOT TO KILL

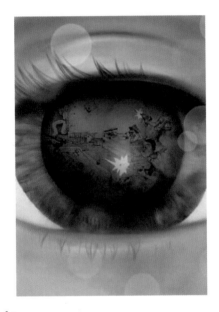

He slowly raises his arm
His hand starts to shake,
Trying to remain calm
But any moment he may break,
A droplet of sweat falls to the ground
As he bites down on his lip
Deep breathing is the only sound,
As the other tightly grips

He points the gun forward
Looks his victim straight in the eye,
He's got him cornered
Tells him
"Today you're going to die,"
"You're a lying, cheating piece of shit that I will not forgive"
"You've tried to control me too many times and I cannot forget,"

"You think you know it all"
"You have to always have your way"
"You've never given a fuck about me or listened to what I have to say,"
"You've only ever cared about you fulfilling you and your selfish needs,"
"I hope the bullet hurts and the wound seriously bleeds"

No longer will you dictate the way I act
No longer will you get inside my head,
You sat there watching as I cracked
Now this is where the path has led,
"I'm talking to you, you worthless fuck"
He aims
And starts to snigger,
"I've let you have your final say"
As he pulls back on the trigger,

BANG

CRAAAAAAAAAAAAAASH

Shattered glass,

Mirror mirror on the wall
I can no longer see you anymore,
This was your total recall
As his image shatters against the floor,
Something much greater will fill that void,
This is the moment
His ego was destroyed,

It's a terrible fight between two wolves
One is EVIL
He is-
Anger, envy, sorrow, regret, greed, arrogance, inferiority, self-pity, guilt,
resentment, lies, false pride, superiorit

DOMESTIC SILENCE

It began with beauty
Kindness and charm
I don't think in his mind he would ever want to harm,
It went on for years as their love went by
But it started getting sketchy
And they didn't know why,

His temper would flair up like she'd never seen before
He got up close
Confronted her
And laid down the law,

He'd start out saying "I'm joking"
As he put on a disguise
But he didn't do very well though

Because she could still see the venom in his eyes
She knew it, lies
She'd been brought up wise,

He then got possessive reading her phone,
Just as she went to the shops
Leaving her home,
He'd say
"Who the fuck's this guy Dave you've been texting?"
She'd say
"You know my dad's called Dave baby you better be messing,"
He then decided to confiscate the car,
Saying
"Where have you got to go?"
"The shops are only so far"
It wasn't long until the bruises started to show
But

Shhhhhhhhh

She had to keep it down low,
Because she didn't want people to know what a cruel beast he was
being
He had a slight suspicion people wouldn't be agreeing
When they were at friends' houses they'd all be laughing and playing
along,
But she had to be on constant guard in case she said something
wrong,

One night
He'd been on her Facebook and seen a message from a guy called
'Dan ,'
Ohhhh
Not a smart move
I don't think I've seen an angrier man,

21

She came downstairs
He quickly gave chase
He got up close with his hot breath in her face,
He grabbed her by the neck and said "Bitch you better explain"
"Who the fuck's this guy Dan why don't I know his name?"
He said he would kill her if she didn't start to speak
But this time she wouldn't take it
She knew he was weak,
She pushed him with every last ounce of energy she still had inside,
She needed a place to get away
She needed a place to hide,
She grabbed an ashtray
And launched with will,
She darted out the house
As he lay there still,

These are the early stages of domestic violence acts,
2 women are killed weekly by domestic violence and these are the facts
1 in 4 women in England experience domestic violence in their life,
It must not amount to the point of a knife,
If your fella has a problem with you going out for the day,
It's him that needs to sort his shit out
Not the other way,
He can't ask you "who you textin'?" every time you're on your phone
Tell him he can back off and to leave you well alone,
Don't let him lay down the law
That prevents you from seeing your friends anymore,

Abuse is not love
Abuse is control

LOST

He stares sharply
She looks lost
He bites bitterly
She whimpers worried
He demands drastically
She freezes fast
He hits hard
She cries carefully
He apologises abruptly
She looks lost
He cries woefully
She looks lost
He kisses kind-heartedly
She looks lost
He forgets
She looks lost

WILL THE PAIN EVER DIE (part 1)

He sits there every night,
Putting on a brave smile and trying to fight
Back the tears he's holding,
As the pain starts scolding,

Wondering

If the pain will ever die   or   if there's a heaven in the sky

He was only 14
He was a bright young kid,
His G.C.S.E's were coming up so
Had a predicament as he'd fallen amid,
The pressure of exams and bullies too,
He sat there in the lonely school ground just wondering what to do,
The bullying started a long time ago,

He tried to tell people but they didn't really want to know,
They said
"darn't worry it'll come and it'll go"
"Just focus on your exams keep it down low,"
So he did

He just wondered

If the pain will ever die   or   if there's a heaven in the sky
He might have a few extra pounds from the rest
But he's just a kid and he's trying his best,
He's got spots on his face
And braces too,
But what they don't know is
He's a musical genius and artist too,
He sits there in lesson
Silent
As quiet as a mouse,
Waiting to run home and get back to the house,
He gets back to the house shuts and locks his door,
There's a battle in his mind it's a constant war,
And all he wants to know is

If the pain will ever die   or   if there's a heaven in the sky

The pain he's been feeling,
Doesn't seem to be healing,
He gets on the floor hands together starts kneeling,
He asks God why he deserves to feel like this
Living every day in agonising abyss,
And all those around just seem to remiss and dismiss,
A tear trickles down his face as his fists clench up tight
For far far too long he has put up a fight,
And all he wants to know is

If the pain will ever die   or   if there's a heaven in the sky

He thought about getting himself a gun,
But he's 14 where's he going to get a gun from?
He said to himself he'd go on the run,
And laughed for a minute because it sounded like fun,
But run where to be exact?
He's got no connections or survival skills and that is just fact,
So he sat there for a minute - feeling - lost and alone,
His heart felt like it had set into stone,
Because the answers he was looking for were completely unknown,
And all he wanted to know is

If the pain will ever die   or   if there's a heaven in the sky

He lay there on his bed,
Coincidentally
He noticed a full pack of paracetamols at the side of his head,
And
Without a second thought he gulps the pack down,
Because he couldn't take it anymore
Acting the class's unwanted clown,
So he sits
And he waits
And he shakes
And he shakes

Wondering

If the pain will ever die   or   if there's a heaven in the sky

Thank god
For the paramedics fighting to keep him alive,
He woke up in the hospital
With his mother at his bed side,

One of the lucky few
Who managed to survive,

Far too young for heaven
Far too young to die,
now looking up
Rather than down
From the sky.

WHAT IS BEAUTY AT SCHOOL?

At primary school a year 5 student came up to me and asked
"Am I beautiful?"
With this huge grin of childlike innocence,
I said… "YES,
YES… you are beautiful,"
And she went…,
"YEEEESSSSSSSSSSS,"
RESULT…
But I feel the answer I gave differed to the answer she heard
You see…
Beauty to me…
Is the moment she helped me find the right classroom after getting lost
in the school's maze,
Beauty was in her brave curious mind,
With a kind, accepting attitude to me and her peers,

The lack of fear in not getting things right, but arm remained prompt
up tight, ready for another attempt,
She was calm and content with respect and willingness to listen,
Courage and driven in any task she was asked to complete,
When I had hand-outs she was the first up out of her seat to offer a
helping hand,
She helped me get back on track to the lesson I'd planned,
Beauty was in her answers to the questions I presented the class...
What does success look like?
"Being happy," she replied,
What is friendship?
"Positivity, trust, love and honesty,"
Honestly, what career would you like to pursue?
"Most people said one that makes me a lot of money," she said, "I want
a job I'm passionate to do,"
I have no doubt her vision looked far past skin, water, muscle and
bone,
She made it her duty no-one was singled out or left alone,
And that's why I said "yes..."
To me... that's what makes you beautiful.

"PLAY"GROUND

I'd never done anything to you
You never even knew my name,
But you found an easy target
To take part in your games,
Your arrow was already drawn
Awaiting your victim,
You knew you
Could handle,

You picked me

I bet
You couldn't believe your luck,
When you laid eyes on
A chubby kid

With trousers that didn't quite fit
Food-stained white top
And to top it off
An unforgiving haircut,

It went on for years
...

Your "play" ground turned into my
No man's land,
Weaving and dodging your shots
Heading for cover
I should have stopped to beg for mercy,
But I didn't know which looked more hopeless
Begging or running away...
Until one day
I'll never forget that day,
The day
I turned my fears to tears,
But this time
They were not mine,

That morning
The first dog I ever knew was being put to sleep,
Mum and Dad deliberated whether
Or not to send me to school,
I made the final decision to go
Unusual for me I know,
But I didn't want to be at home,
Where a family member was dying

I'd been through the gates around
15 minutes
Until a voice called over
Piercing my ear drums

"oi fat boy"
I heard him say

Quickly I responded
"NOT TODAY"

I turned around,
My eyes welled up
As red as the blood that was soon to spill,

"Don't tell me what to do"
He demanded

But he knew I wasn't backing down today

Suddenly

I flew
Towards him

A frenzy unravelling in gravel,
Friends and enemies holla from the rabble,
Jab the body, grab a collar,
In one foul swing,
I break his nose,
It explodes across his face,
I throw again
Again, again, again
Again, again and again
Then
A teacher comes to pull me away,
I squirm
Scream and say,
"I'll kill you, I've had enough I'll take no more"
As his body lay motionless across

The "play"ground floor

It terrifies me
To this day
The long-term damage I could have inflicted on that boy,
I don't like pain,
It's never been my aim to hurt,
I'm not a fighter,
I don't think fighting is right,
But there is so much someone can take,
Until they
Either break
Or
Make a move,

If you beat a dog into a corner
Get ready to be bitten.

Like You

I love like you,
I laugh like you,
I want somebody just like you do,
I anger like you,
I get rage like you,
I bleed the same colour of blood just like you do,
I grieve like you,
I fear like you,
I don't want to lose just like you,
So why are you trying so hard to hurt me?
Is it because you don't like me?
Or you don't like you?

MAN'S BEST FRIEND

Quite a home we have made,
Many memories I shall save,
Fast feet, tasty treat,
Truly you are...man's best friend

Carefree whatever the weather brings,
Enjoying all your surroundings,
Broken furniture, I shall mend,
Truly you are... man's best friend

Eyes begging me not to go out,
I don't recall a single fallout,
Broken rules, I let you bend,
Truly you are...man's best friend

We share my dinner but never yours
Jump on my bed without a pause,
Never angry, can't even pretend,
Truly you are…man's best friend

Walk side by side
Each other as a guide
Often getting lost
Absorbing the countryside

Always in the moment
With the time we spend
Truly you are…man's best friend
Sat with me on the darkest nights
Looking at me saying "it'll be alright"
You were there till the bitter end
Truly you are…man's best friend

You're the only one that never walked away
Listened to everything I had to say,
Sadly missed, pain I couldn't comprehend
Truly you are…man's best friend.

Troll

I was raised by my grandmother,
A kind-hearted, tender, compassionate lady with a beautiful wise side,
She'd read to me and my older sister for hours,
Books, fables and tales were told,
SO
Seeing you act the way you do makes me wonder how you became so
cold,
Have you ever experienced a fairy tale?
Did no-one ever read to you?
I wonder if they did, would it have changed the way you act?
Because if you did you'd know it's a well-documented fact,
The bad guy
NEVER comes out on top,
If you stop before the climax of the tale you lose the moral,
But the bad character is always the loser;
Hansel and Gretel burnt the evil witch alive,
Three little pigs turned the wolf to dinner,
Cinderella's beauty finds the prince and the ugly hearts are left with
nothing,
To not guide yourself from these stories,

To pick the path and follow the footsteps of the troll,
To stay closed off in your dark, confined space,
Behind a screen awaiting your victims,
Is to never see what lies on the other side of the bridge,
Or taste the happily ever after,
You're after.

5 NATURAL

EMOTIONS

Emotions running everywhere
Emotions running high

Emotions are the reasons

We laugh and we cry

Emotions are natural
That is a fact

But it's important not to repress them

It's kind of a

B   L   N   I   G
A   A   C   N
Act

Emotions are there to motivate us
To help us achieve our goals,

When we try and hide them it can be painful and destructive
So we must learn the controls,

It's time to master getting wet
Absorbing the rain
Because avoiding emotions
Buys you short-term gain,
At the price of long-term pain

5 natural emotions   -

Grief
The emotion that allows us to say goodbye
To those we couldn't imagine letting go
It's fundamental you feel the sadness
It helps you build and grow,
Left repressed
Grief turns to depression
It will hit you hard in the end
Going through tough times?
It's okay to feel tender
If you let yourself feel you'll mend,

Anger
It allows you to say "NO"
And stand up for yourself when your back is against the wall
It doesn't have to be abusive or damaging to anyone
It's your call if it ends in a brawl,
Left repressed
Anger turns to rage
You'll feel imprisoned and ready to roar
Like a lion trapped in a cage,

Envy
It motivates you
And helps you climb to the top,

The moment you begin to ruthlessly push down others
Learn to relax and stop.
Left repressed
Envy turns to jealousy
This will destroy you
And push those you love far away
Let this emotion drive you forward
But don't let negative thoughts stray,

Fear
It's a huge part to play in evolution and survival
It allows us to feel alive
This emotion is not our rival,
Left repressed
Fear turns to panic
This can completely prevent you living
And will soon break you down,
It's okay to dip your toes in the water
Just be smart enough
Not to drown,

Love
This is our strongest emotion …
Where there is love
There is life
Left repressed
Love turns to possessiveness
This will cut your soul
Like a knife.

It's so important we learn to feel our emotions
And not keep pushing them elsewhere
The more you feel
The more you heal
And slowly begin to repair.

"NEWS"

Live in fear – drink some beer
See some tits on page 3 here

IMMIGRATION KILLING THE NATION
BE TERRIFIED OF THE HOODIE GENERATION

Support the Tories they know best
Don't ask questions we'll do the rest

Build bigger barriers and lock your doors
What are you on about illegal wars?

Fear benefit cheats they're taking out streets
Here look at these half price meats

Here's a black man with a gun

Be fearful of him he's on the run

Fracking is cracking
Money is lacking
So yet again
You've got it
The Tories you should be backing

God save the queen we need her alive
Without her how could we possibly survive?

People on drugs are mindless thugs
Down with hippies and their compassion and hugs,

Global warming is an elaborate lie
Forget about the Ozone in the sky

A paedophile may take your child
Be scared of the world BECAUSE THE WORLD'S GONE
WILD

Don't worry though

We have some materials you may want to get
Here's paddy power come on place your bet
Nice shiny car you could own
You'll feel better but probably need a loan
We just want you to feel more at ease
We love you all we just aim to please.

SMILE

S   E

M   L

I

It's happiness and it's right under your nose,
It's a curve that sets everything straight,
A warm smile is the universal language of kindness so let's start now,
there's no need to wait,

Sometimes your joy is the source of your smile,
But sometimes your smile can be the source of your joy,
Struggling to find it?
Remember my friend it's just a choice when you want to deploy,
And o boy,

44

When you find it,
It's the brightest light to keep your mind lit,

PEACE
Literally begins with a smile,
So smile because it happened don't cry because it's over,
For some reason
For some people
A smile on the face is as rare as a four-leaf clover,
If you're reading this,
CONGRATULATIONS YOU'RE ALIVE!
ISN'T THAT SOMETHING WE CAN ALL AGREE TO SMILE
ABOUT,
Sorry didn't mean to shout
Just wanted to get rid of your doubt
And help your cheeks shine out,
If the world's a veil of tears,
Smile till rainbows span it,
Try and get all your smiles in now before the government try and ban
it,
(Seriously I wouldn't put it past them)
If you feel you're falling under,
A kind look   a gentle word   a good-natured smile
Can accomplish miracles and really works wonders,
It's the one way to fight back from the aggressive lightning and heavy
thunders,
So
If you want to keep your head above the ground,
Let us meet with a smile
For the smile is the beginning of love I've found.

It was Saturday night and they were out on the town
They got to the pub and they knocked a few down,
There was banter there the night did seem fun
But they got to the club and the madness begun,

He had a fake ID because he was 17
But he was with the older lads so he knew the routine,
He'd get near the back they'd all move around
He'd get past the bouncer
It was easy
It was sound,

The music was pumping
The guys started hunting
Looking around at the pretty girls jumping,
He'd had 8 Jaeger bombs it was around 11
He'd be dancing with a girl

Who looked like she'd fallen from heaven,
But she moved to another guy
Giving her the eye
And he didn't take it too kindly as he
Waved her goodbye,
He went to the bar and smashed 2 more jaegers down his neck
Then he went to the bathroom because he was feeling a wreck,
The toilet was dirty
He got piss on his feet
As he noticed 2 lads
Snorting coke off a seat,
It was his mates that he'd gone with Adam and Tom
So they gave him a line
And his mind was just gone,
He'd spent around £100 at this point of the night
He was feeling pretty restless and he wanted a fight,
He remembered the lad that took his bird
So he went to find him
And give him a word,
He tapped him on the shoulder
He grabbed his shirt
There was a look in his face of violence and hurt,
He slapped him in the face said "what you gonna do?"
"Let's go outside yeah
Just me and you"

They were mindless and drunk rolling on the floor
All his mates were gathered round chanting
"MORE MORE MORE",
Someone from the crowd shouted "please just stop it"
"He's clearly had enough he just wants to drop it,"
But the alcohol and adrenaline had really started to affect
So any rational thought he just had to reject,
They both got together

They threw all they had,
They both fell to the ground
This could only end bad,
But then they both stopped
As one gave out a yelp,
There was a puddle of blood on his jacket
And he was screaming for help!

Now

I don't want to say which guy died that night
It's up for you to decide who won the fight,
Just know there were a lot of lives affected
That will never be the same
Because of this war on the street and this knife crime game,
There's a broken mother
Who's lost a little boy
Because one of the lads thought a knife was a toy,
They both had very promising lives ahead
Now ones facing prison
And
The other is dead,
There were 30,000 recorded offences involving knives that year
But don't let this statistic hit you with fear,
We just need to elevate our minds and change the way we value others
See everyone in our community as part of our brothers

WHEN WE MEET AGAIN

Lungs made for laughter
With a heart pure as love,
Veins run true of fire and passion
A smile of innocence
Mind full of confidence and memories,
We shall share,
When we meet again

Your arms invited all in
With warmth in your chest,
Eyes that only saw beauty
Ears that listened with care,
Hands full of trust,
We shall hold,
When we meet again

Your lungs got weak,
But your laughter remained
Your heart slowed down
But your love stayed the same,
Your veins were frail,
But your fire never stopped burning,
Your warmth I will miss,
Until we meet again

JOHANNESBURG (WHITE BOY)

"What you doin' 'ere den white boy?"
"We not got many of you around dees parts"
"It's a very dangerous place for a white face 'round 'ere"
"As soon as you get off dis bus follow me"
"Don't talk to anybody and don't make eye contact, ok?"

I looked to my right side with what started as fear,
Immediately met with terror as a dead body entered my vision,
This was all me and my decision to board the bus,
So I just had to sit tight
And ride out the situation.

"You see dat?"
"Dat dead body has been der a long time"
"You know why?"

He looks me dead in the eye,
"If you try an' move the body den it's your responsibility"
"Nobody want dat on der hands"
"So dey just walk by"
"Let it hit rigamortis."

I sit up stiff,
Held on to my seat,
Felt I'd sealed my own fate,
Succumbed to defeat, to the situation.

The only option I had left,
Was to trust this stranger,
Let him guide me to safety,
Those around me sensed my discomfort,
I felt alien,
Like a toothpaste mark on a clean black top,

The bus came to a stop.

"'Ere, come on now follow me"
"I'll tek you to de taxi rank,"

"Tha.."
"Don't thank me just follow."

The night was on its way,
As the doors opened,

I was swarmed right to left,

Left to right,

Not another white face in sight,
This has never mattered to me,
But here,
It meant everything.

Shouts and calls from passers-by,
"Why you 'ere white boy?"
"Where you going white boy?"
"You got money white boy?"
"Come over 'ere white boy."

"Come with me"
The stranger demanded,
"Don't give 'em any of ya money"
"Da taxi is not too far away."

"I.. I… I've not actually got the funds to pay"

"'Ere."

He puts 50 rand in my hand,

We arrive at the taxis,
He tells me to get in,
Lock the door,

Two drivers have a punch up,
Winner takes all,
A man knocks at my window asking for money,
I pretend I'm taking a call,
Watch the battle unfold,
My driver
Holds the other against the bonnet,
SHOUTS
"HE'S MY CUSTOMER NAH STAY DE FUCK BAK,"
He climbs in the front,
We head off back to the hostel.

The next day I fly out of Johannesburg,
And we never
Meet again.

STICKS AND STONES

From hunting food and carving rocks,
To suit and tie... watching clocks,
From picking fruit and gathering sticks,
To mass corruption politics...
Where are we heading,
It's doing my head in,
Sticks and stones,
Now breaking bones,

We used to be satisfied with our basic rules,
We learnt to carve rocks to make our tools,
We needed to grow so we built the schools,
Then conditioned intellectual fools...,
We'd find meat to eat and wood to burn,
Learning to survive was our main concern,

Now our main concern is that we mainly earn,
Money is power that we're made to learn...,
Find things to do just to fill the time,
Then made a hierarchy we needed to climb...,
Invented language for a better understanding,
But with the power we became demanding...,
We made the wheel so came the horse and cart,
A faster mode of transport it was a perfect start,
But with the rapid changes man got smart,
And we discovered we could kill man with a poisoned dart...,
In order to find new islands we designed boats and rafts,
To keep track of where we were going we developed our maps...,
Found remedies from trees that could cure disease,
Then realised disease could make the pennies...,
Instead of treating the ill we were making them ill,
Then sending them back with a medical bill.

From hunting food and carving rocks,
To suit and tie... watching clocks,
From picking fruit and gathering sticks,
To mass corruption politics...,
Where are we heading,
It's doing my head in,
Sticks and stones,
Now breaking bones,

Once the travel began we created nation,
With the ideology of nation came more confrontation...,
Assembled soldiers and built our forces,
Extra demand ate up recourses...,
Tank and machine gun replaced the horse,
We wiped out races with no remorse...,
In the soil we found oil at a costly price,
Take what we could left to our own devices...,

Manipulate nutrition lie about what we require,
Whatever could be mass made sent the profits higher,
Death... illness... disease
Spread like wildfire,
But keep pumping it out to you...
the buyer...,
As soon as it was our turn to fly,
We learnt to drop the big bomb from the sky,
Made certain rules and regulations we must comply,
If not met threat civilians would die...,
I know I may have simplified our evolutionary tale,
But lack of simplicity is where we did fail...,
If you're looking for solutions we must calm the mind,
Evolve the heart,
Slow things down and look back to the start.

From hunting food and carving rocks,
To suit and tie... watching clocks,
From picking fruit and gathering sticks,
To mass corruption politics...,
Where are we heading,
It's doing my head in,
Sticks and stones,
Now breaking bones,

Where are we heading,
It's doing my head in,
Sticks and stones,
Now breaking bones,

Where are we heading,
It's doing my head in,
Sticks and stones,
Now breaking bones.

ROUND THE CORNER

The only thing we have that's constant is change,
What's round the corner isn't for us to see,
We must always expect the unexpected apparently…
Introducing Chris, 19 years old,
On his way to university with a mind of ambition and heart full of gold,
"Life was stressful to begin with I couldn't keep myself out of mischief"
"I've never been a nasty lad, just a bit of banter I had, but I've turned a new leaf,"
"I needed to clean my act up to try and pursue my passion in sport,"
"I want to be a basketball player but they say I'm too short,"
"That's ok though I'll give anything a go,"
"I'll put my all in, push myself, in my mind I will grow,"
"I'm excited to see what my future brings it looks good, bright and clear,"

"But where exactly I'm going"
"Well… I have no idea,"
"Just going for it, curious and free"
Because "**what's round the corner isn't for us to see,**"
"**We must always expect the unexpected apparently**"
"That's the best bit of advice my mum always gave me…"

Introducing Lucy 23 years young,
Beautiful girl treating everyday like spring has sprung,
"I always have a smile on my face and why wouldn't I?"
"I enjoy what I do, put my all into anything that I try,"
"I'm thinking of traveling the world soon not sure where I'm going
or how I'm going get there,"
"But that doesn't faze me at all I don't really care,"
"Because if you don't know where you're heading any road will take
you there,"
"I flow with the universe and adapt when needs be",
"Because you see,
 "**Life's strange**"
"**The only thing we have that's constant is change**"
"That's the best advice my father's ever given to me…"

Introducing Linda 60 years of age,
A bubbly entertaining woman who sees life as her stage,
"Life is a dance I take it day by day,"
"Always staying strong ready for what may come my way,"
"Have a loving supportive family but it's not always been easy,"
"My children are finding their feet 'thank god' which is starting to
please me,"
"My youngest always knew how to get in the bad books,"
"He never failed to make me laugh though with his charms and
good looks,"
I'm excited to what the future brings positivity is key",
"Because **what's round the corner isn't for us to see,**"

"We must always expect the unexpected apparently"
"That's what my dad always use to tell me…"

Introducing Mark, 43,
The absolute joker of the pack everyone would agree,
"In my opinion a day without laughter is a day that's been wasted,"
"I just enjoy spending my time around plenty smiling faces,"
"A good laugh to me helps cure a lot of heart ache,"
"It slows things down when all you need is a break," "Life is short
and reality is what you make it,"
"You only get one go around I think so you may as well take it,"
"I haven't had an easy life lost my wife back last year,"
"I'm often reminded about it still live in fear,"
"I'll fall through the trap door,"
"Taste love once more,"
"I've never dealt with emotions of that magnitude before,"
"Just my kids I live for now I'm their guide and mentor,"
 I tell them…
"Life's strange"
"The only thing we have that's constant is change,"
You see
"That's the advice my mother always gave me…"

Now…

Introducing you to PC Grey,
"I've got the duty of informing a mother and father their child won't
be coming back today,"
"One's in a cell waiting to hear what the police have to say,"
"And ones in a hospital bed,"
"But her soul has slipped away…"
What will it take,
To learn to break,
And slow down?

Comes at a hell of a cost,
Too many lives lost,
In this town,
I see too many broken hearts and too many shattered dreams,
But like they say,
Life's Strange...
The only thing we have that's constant is change,
What's round the corner isn't for us to see,
We must always expect the unexpected apparently...

That night Chris was driving back home from work in a hurry,
He forgot to leave the key out and was starting to worry,
He was never usually a dangerous driver,
But this night he lapsed,
For no real reason he was driving too fast,
Not far from his home he was doing 50mph round the bend,
This is the moment Lucy's tale was coming to an end, she was round the corner on her mobile talking,
Oblivious to Chris she just kept on walking,
Chris looked up…
Quickly hitting the break,
But unfortunately
For both of them it was moments too late…
He couldn't slow down fast enough which sealed her fate,
We're now investigating a crime,
And that's how Chris, Lucy, Mark, Linda and so many more stories changed in a moment of time,

What's round the corner isn't for us to see,
We must always expect the unexpected apparently

YOU PULL THE TRIGGER

Guns don't kill people,
People do.
There's a much more important element than gunpowder,
That's you.

The gun doesn't pull the trigger,
The gun just made the spark,
You can't blame the gun for following him in the dark.
The gun doesn't pull the trigger,
The gun just made the sound,
You can't blame the gun for him just lying there on the ground.

Guns don't kill people,
People do.
There's a much more important element than gunpowder,

That's you.

Accept responsibility for your actions

Be accountable for your results

Take ownership of your mistakes

YOU'RE ELEMENTAL

Tirade of abuse,
Useless energy put in to motion,
As emotions pour out

Hollow words blurred fire in your direction,
Shots don't connect you stay calm and don't react,
Facts… thoughts… feelings hurled towards you,
Time goes by and the ammo has run out

Time you know heals and for that you wait quietly,
While we flair up and wait for the fire to roar,
But still and relaxed is your best element…
Our words spout out up in the air,
While you watch them fly by you're so down to earth

You're elemental to our family,

The most inspirational man to me,
Calm the fire… keep us down to earth,
Still the water and clear the air,
You're there

We think we're strong because we know how to shout,
We think we're strong because we won't back down,
But real strength lies deep in your tranquillity,
The ability you've been passed down through peace and love…
You rise above the needless threats and clamour
Don't get drawn in to the clumsy noise,
Poise and balance given to the room
You know it will be over soon
We'll all be friends again,

You're elemental to our family,
The most inspirational man to me,
Calm the fire… keep us down to earth,
Still the water and clear the air,
You're there

Our words turn over to you and somehow blame you,
For the pain and confusion unsettled inside…
But your words rise up in a heated exchange,
Cleverly they know how to change the course of the day,
While my range of words remain hollow and aimless,
But I see each one of them learning from you

You're elemental to our family,
The most inspirational man to me,
Calm the fire… keep us down to earth,
Still the water and clear the air,
You're there.

YIN YANG

So

You've come to a red light,
Your mind's saying turn back
But your heart's saying fight,
You were cruising along,
Everything seemed strong,
Nothing at all could possibly go wrong,
But now your lights started dimming
And you're trapped
In the cave,

RELAX

Don't worry

It's just time to be brave,

Now

There's something troubling you like a splinter in the brain,
Just ask yourself
How would you know joy if you weren't to experience pain?
You right to think your life is precious
So let's make this moment ours,
It's time to focus on the brightest days
But find hope in the darkest hours,
It's funny
While your fire's roaring bright we're happy to let it burn,
But when the cold times come
We don't know where to turn,
Never should you feel you're at the point of no return,
Don't freeze up and turn to ice
Just listen in and learn,

So

Just hear me out here
Let's think about this
Because it's time for enlightening,
I mean
We learn to appreciate the sunshine
Through rain thunder and lightning,
If you sat on a roller coaster
The excitement comes from the ups
And the downs and the turns
And the twists
So just sit back
Stay calm
Let it flow
Loosen your fists.

You feel your falling rapidly and desperate to fly,
But how would you admire the glimmering stars
Without the dark sky,
To enjoy the pleasure of the calm times
The beauty in silence,
You have to of experienced some form of turbulence
Upset and violence,
Would you ever truly understand the glory of success,
If you've never experienced the pain of feeling you've failed?
When you begin the see the importance of balance
The truth is unveiled,
YES
In life there are plenty of tricks,
But let's not forget about the treats,
Because you have to of tasted bitter
To really understand sweet,
There'll be times where you're going to have to deal with loss
But you'll gain again and release all your pain,
So
Don't tip the scale,
Keep the train on the rail,
Stand strong in the gale,
Let the ship peacefully sail,
Take off your mask remove your veil,
Take a deep breath,

Inhale

Exhale

This is the part of your life where you write a new tale,
Ok
The dark times may be here
But it's time to look around,

Because there's peace deep inside you
Just waiting to be found,
Remember
In the dark there is light
There's day there is night
There's black and there's white
Never stay blind
Have vision and sight.

HALF MORAL HIPPIE

Dreadlocks, baggy tops –
Incense shops,
Tree of life on your necklace –
Glittery flower upon your face,
Eye of Horus tattooed on your back –
Non – travelled backpack,
Dream catcher above your bed –
Telling me what Nietzsche said,
Peace symbol on your shoes –
Many political world views,
Indigo Ocean as your Facebook name –
"WE'RE ALL ONE," you exclaim,
The "V" sign on your car bumper –
Alpaca wool rainbow jumper.

Half moral "hippie" you've got all gear,
But what it takes to become a "good person" you're not so clear.

You don't like labels –
I listened while you label her a slag,
You say it's wrong to steal –
I watched you take every last flake inside that bag,
You say debating is good –
I see you roll your eyes when opinion is shared,
When you're receiving –
Is the only time it looked like you cared.

Like a rave in Sheffield,
You don't know what to expect,
Like a badly rolled joint,
You have to reject,
Like a poorly quoted quote,
You struggle to make sense,
Like a terribly beaten sand bag,
Your look is intense,
You give me anger,
I never knew I had,
I'll wait for you to get over
This half moral
Fashion fad.

ARE YOU BEING REAL?

I just want real, yeah
I want the real you
I want the real feel
Real deal
Really real you

Don't cover up your scars
Be proud of who you are
There'll always be cracks, bumps and scratches on a well toured guitar,

I just want real, yeah
I want the real you
I want the real feel
Real deal
Really real you

You've got nothing else to prove
We've got nothing to left to lose...
Maybe together we can learn from our bruises,

I just want real, yeah
I want the real you
I want the real feel
Real deal
Really real you

Explain to me how you're feeling,
Tell me where your head is at,
This is no cat and mouse chase
You will not wind up in a trap,

No hidden agenda here,
Nothing you have to hide,
I want to see the Imperfect, Flawed, Quirky, Weird, Beautiful, Magical
Person deep inside

Because...
I just want real, yeah
I want the real you
I want the real feel
Real deal
Really real you

NICE GUY AT HEART (PART 3)

He was just 18 when he went to jail
He got 5 years when he went off the rail,
At school everybody knew his name
Bedding girls was part of his game
He was a loud mouth with only one aim
Getting to the top
Climbing to the fame,
And glory
Because he was chasing a story,
Of what he was told to pursue
No matter what he had to do,

He had every new gadget you'd ever seen
His mind was filthy
But his looks were clean,

He knew all the talk to the gangster slang
He use to go around town and do his "thang,"
He wasn't too afraid of fighting either
I've heard of a story where he held up a guy with a cleaver,
(True story)
He used to do drugs for a quiet night in,
But the night he went off the rails
That was the beginning of him,

As he got to the prison ground
Everybody gathered around,
He was acting cocky
He was acting hard
But he knew he wasn't safe and sound,
But he put on a front though
Fair play to him
But he wasn't too cocky as he took one on the chin,
He got back up,
He gives him a dirty look,
Says
"What the fuck,"
BOOM
Back down,
He'd been there 5 hours
He'd broke his nose and cracked his eye
That's the moment his reputation did die,
From then on he knew it would be a hard time in the nick
But 6 months later things did start to click,
He met an old bloke that had been there a while
He was helping him out he was making him smile,
One day the old guy gave him a poem he'd wrote
He said really read it
Really take note...

74

The poem

I was like you
Just a young ruthless lad,
I'd get myself in any opportunity where mischief could be had,
I had girls   Rolex   BM'S   the lot
But happiness is one thing I never really got,
Since my time here I've been really doing some thinking
Being really true
My emotions have started to sink in,
Every single night I have to think about the people I affected
Not just the one victim
But the others closely connected,
I hear the screams squeaks squeals in my head
Most nights I wish I was the one that was dead,
Listen boy
Don't end up like me
Liberate your soul and set yourself free,
Life is a movie
You can pick what character you are
Don't be the wanabe scar face that always takes it too far,
Life is magic
You've got the stick don't be an arsehole led by your dick,
Life's like labyrinth
You're part of a maze
Come on man it's time to change your ways,
You're so
So young
Life's still so free,
Choose your next moves carefully
Don't end up like me.

WE STAND STRONG TOGETHER

You were there for me when they tried to section me
You told them I'd be alright,
You were there for me when I got kicked out the hostel
We stayed on that beach all night,
You wrestled that guy
Blackened his right eye
We stand strong together

You were there for me when I tripped up hard
Said you'd protect me be my bodyguard,
You were there for me when she walked away
Said it'd be okay take it day by day,
Somehow you turn everything into a joke
Make the bad days fade away like smoke,
We stand strong together

You are there for me no matter what
You bring the ice when times get hot,
You are the penalty spot
You're still there when I miss the shot,
You are there I'll never forget
No matter how old you're my first tape cassette,
Together we make a harmonious duet,
Keep days light like a warm sunset

FALLING

Life's one big road with lots of signs
Let your inner light shine

Ego's ego's ego's mad you know
Ego's ego's ego's mad

I found vision in the I

It's funny how smooth the surface was
But
I didn't see the hole in the ground,
I was too busy looking up at the clouds
I forgot to take a look down,

The phone call I received that day
Was the moment I started to fall,
Screamed and shouted on my way down

But knew no one would answer my call,
One missed step
Suddenly
Darkness was my vision
It came out of nowhere
Completely out my control
I had no part to play in the decision,

Momentum from the fall quickly started to build
I couldn't deal with the pace
Lost in the cosmos
Total abyss
Gliding through time and space,

Noise
CHATTER
All around
I
Struggled
Panicked
Cried

Tried to reach the sides
Arms stretched wide,
But
Nothing was stopping me
Slowing me down

Substances dragged into the equation
It gets darker
Darker
Darker
Suddenly
Turns pitch black
Realise the pit is becoming bottomless

And there ain't no turning back,

Line… to tab… to toke to toke
Mega bucks
To flat out broke,
A new body would share my bed
Each day of the week
I was weak…
Couldn't bear the thought of an empty bed,
"How could anybody want to share my warmth again?"
Was a loop inside my head,

Made an abundance of friends in the space of weeks
Thinking that'll set me free,
What I didn't realise
The friend I truly needed to love
Was ultimately…
Me

Ego's ego's ego's mad you know
Ego's ego's ego's mad

Still Falling
Down
In
Direction
DON'T LOOK IN THE MIRROR YOU'LL HATE YOUR
REFLECTION
Mad where the mind takes you with fear of rejection,
Self
Reality
I couldn't connect
Vision distorted
Patterns formed
Terrified

Hopeless
Suffering the storm,
Until a voice called out
I felt all
tingly and warm,

"Slow…slow…now stop"
"The more you fight and struggle you'll never find your way back to the top,"

I begged
"WELL HELP ME…GUIDE ME THE WAY"
"WHERE AM I GOING WRONG?"

The voice replied
"No more asking questions join in with the dance and peacefully become part of the song"

SUDDENLY

BANG

TAZER…TAZER…TAZER

BANG

Hit the floor

Ouch shit
That hurt
Like a pain I'd never felt before,
The pit did have a bottom
To get back to the top was going to be a hell of a climb,
It was never going to be a simple mission
I just had to bide my time,

Pick myself up

Dust myself off

cough

Look around

Gaze up

I know there's only one way to go

Look up in the distance
Like a lightbulb there's nirvana
Flaming in constant glow,

REMEMBER
If you're ever in the pit
The ground is always coming up,
It gives you time to reflect on yourself
And refill your cup,
Knowledge there's a bottom
Removes complete despair
Let it become a challenge
Not a nightmare
There'll be days you are clueless and don't know what to do
But faith is why I'm here today
Faith is why I made it through,
Experiencing the dark can come at quite a cost
You'll lose the world
But gain the universe
When you swim in the sea of the lost,

Ego's ego's ego's mad you know
Ego's ego's ego's mad

LYING WITH ME

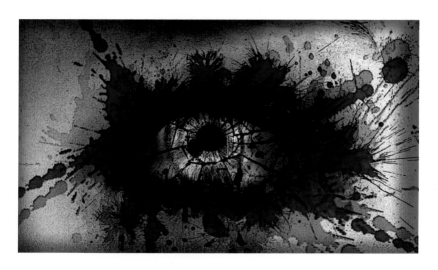

When I'm lying with you I feel free
But I can't stand when you're lying with me,
You get cross and angry when I question you
Then upset with me when I find out the truth,
I'm puzzled by people confused in your poker face,
But I feel the joker as I keep giving chase,
It must be lust that holds me tight,
I honestly don't trust you and you've proved me right,
It's wrong to think that this is easily forgotten,
But I'm far too scared to tell you to jog on,
So I sit us down and say let's talk,
Instead of turning you around and telling you to walk,

Nothing tells the truth like a lie,
But I can't stand watching you cry,

Why is it I don't like goodbyes,

What is it about that look in your eyes?
Back and forth back and forth
Push and shove,
You say that you're in love but your words are disguised,
The glove doesn't fit
I don't want to hear more lies,
Because I spy with my little eye something strange going on,
It's up in the air you don't seem to care
now what are we running from?
Tell me you want a lover,
there's been a fair few,
Why are you waiting on another,
This dream will never come true...

Nothing tells the truth like a lie,
But I can't stand there watching you cry,

Hang on though I'm the real fool here,
You know every time a tear falls,
It's me who ends up apologising,
Sympathising for how you feel,
reassuring you that's it's no big deal,
Are you really going to let me pick up the pieces?
When you brought in the weaponry?
It's me scrambling on my knees in shattered glass,
I'm just hurting myself
But I can't let it pass,
Say this is the last time it can't happen again,
Then you come in my arms and we're already friends,
Freeing my mind,
Every time you look find,
An excuse
A reason that it went this way,
For some reason all I can say,

"don't worry everything will be ok,"

Nothing tells the truth like a lie,
But I can't stand there watching you cry,

WHATS RIGHT?

...or do you do what's wrong to do what's right

Should you Jump the pearly gates or wait,

Well...

Antony Bates was arrested
Far too many times,
For far too many reasons to mention,
A rebel without a cause for a while He liked the grand theft auto life style,
His story grabbed my attention,
Anthony use to steal ... He saw himself as the modern day Robin Hood,
Career criminal with a family to feed you see, so he'd get what he could,

He would have tried getting a job to earn a real honest way of living,
But when you have a record as long as your arm not many employers really want to give him,
The opportunity he needed,
So he did,
Pick a pocket or 2 or 3,
Not from the people mainly corporate companies,
The last crime he committed was for aggravated assault,
The man who mugged his mother was found and beaten to a pulp,
As a result he was sentenced back inside without hesitation,
But He decided he wasn't staying around this time to last the duration,
There was too much to play for on the outside of the cage and locks,
So he wasn't just going to be taken in and confined by the cops,

Do you do what's right?
Or do you do what's wrong to do what's right?

Anthony's mother was battling for her life with deteriorating health,
If Anthony missed her passing he wouldn't be able to live with himself,
She was bedridden in their family home diagnosed with rare form of cancer,
Sometimes the only answer we're left with,
When a loved one's name is on the death list
Is to head for the exits and find any way home…
There was no menacing intention in his decision,
To break out of the prison,
He just needed to be around while his mum was still living,
She's the only person that's ever cared for him from the beginning till the end,
Guardian, protector, defender and his best friend,
Late at night he climbed his way onto the roof and scaled the prison wall,

Took a hell of a fall,
To freedom with a long way to go,
Anthony wasn't left just running from cops,
Antony was now racing the clock,

Do you do what's right?
Or do you do what's wrong to do what's right?

He hot-wired a car a couple miles down the road,
Knew exactly what he needed to do and turned to flight mode,
Every time he heard the faint sound of wailing sirens or saw blue flashing lights,
He did all he could to keep out of sight,
Taking the back roads,
Changing clothes,
Keeping a low profile traveling town to town,
Meanwhile the police were hunting him down,
Cat and mouse had truly begun,
The media escalated the situation terrifying everyone,
"LOCK YOUR DOORS, HIDE INSIDE, THERE'S A MONSTER ON THE RUN,"
But Anthony had no other motive then to get to his dying mum,
He wasn't going to stop until his objective was done,
Around 10pm the police found a stolen BM on a farm,
Only kilometres away from his destination,
During the investigation,
There'd been reports around that raised the alarm the farm was his resting station,
A description of a man that fit bill had been spotted near some old sheds out the way,
The police sprinted round the back on the trail to their prey,
This hunt was moments from being complete,
They burst through the door screaming,
"GET ON THE FLOOR, GET ON THE FLOOR!"

But Anthony wasn't there anymore and the cops had been beat,

He'd made it to his mother 4 hours before,
Holding her hand while she died,
He had no idea what the next steps would be,
It didn't matter to him however,
He got to say his final goodbye,

Do you do what's right?
Or do you do what's wrong to do what's right?

WE

We give, we get
We fall, we fight
We pull, we push
With all our might
We laugh, we cry
We hurt, we bite
We must never
Lose our sight,
We worry, we think
We think, we think
We let
Our ship
Sink

We lose   we learn   till our next turn
We don't matter
We are matter

LOVE IS ALL WE SHARE

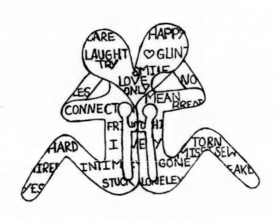

It's gone past caring
I mean she'll be flaring up every time I enter the room,
Spooning times are gone now,
How did it come to this?
I miss our laughter
But it seems the fact of the matter is…
The stitching has torn,
Sew
Love is the only thing we seem to have in common
And the common denominator is…
We don't know who we are anymore,
Worked too hard on becoming a two
Loves got us stuck together like glue,
I don't mean to blame you…
I don't mean to blame me…

But this is supposed to be
easy

We're holding our hands too tightly
Each day ever so slightly
We're pulling in a different direction
We still have our love
But we've lost our connection

If life's a game of cards we're playing 52 pickup,
It's more than a hiccup
Lungs are overworking and we've lost our breath
Less intimacy
And we've missed a step,
What fool begins a marathon and starts off in a sprint,
We've grown tired of each other
And my pockets are skint,
But there's a glint in your eye
That won't allow me to say goodbye
I don't know why,
But you hardly even know me and it's starting to show that
I hardly even know you
And I don't like what I know,

Now this is proving a test in my quest for happiness,
I'm trying to think less,
But I don't know the best road to take
Do we try?
Or
Do we break?
If it works
Is it fake?
The odds are up but what's the stake,
(T bone or not T bone that is the question)

I guess we just wait and take things slow
Because impulsivity is in my nature,
No I don't hate ya,
But this can't carry on
The load's too heavy
I'm feeling the strain,
This train's on a beaten track
I'm not sure if we can bring it back.

STOP-LISTEN-START

Stop   listen   start

You spend your whole life trying to realise your worth,
But you've always been more than enough
Ever since your birth,
You question yourself every single step you take,
You never have faith anymore
In any move that you make,
It's time my friend to

STOP   LISTEN   START

STOP
Sorting everyone else's problems
Till you've sorted out what's going on in that head of yours,
STOP

Hanging around with people that only pick out all your flaws,
STOP
Hating
STOP
Creating
all these problems you've made,
STOP
Holding onto anger and the pain will soon fade,
STOP
Clinging to that girl who only has ethics and morals when she chooses
to play along,
Yes it's wrong! You've got to be strong,
STOP
Neglecting yourself your health, body and needs
This is the first place where pain really feeds,
STOP
Aiming for perfection just aim to do your best,
STOP
Fighting constantly through stressed times
Sometimes just give it a rest,
STOP
Chasing for happiness, your life doesn't need to be rigid
Always under control,
Just let things go
It's good for your soul,
STOP
Waiting around for someone else to make you a happier you
Here are a few ideas of what you can START to do,
START
Figuring out your biggest time wasters and energy drainers
Let them take a back seat,
START
Finding people out there like fountains
There's plenty to meet,

START
Waking up and telling yourself today
Is going to be good!
Happiness isn't something that just happens in childhood,
START
To smile and laugh more, life really is too short,
It's not your fault you forget this
But in school it's to pass tests and exams what were taught,
IF
You're going to compare
START
To compare yourself to yourself
How much have you grown?
How far have you come?
Have you progressed to your goals and dreams?
If so
What have you done?
START
To truly appreciate family
It doesn't matter how big your house is
It just matters that there's love there inside,
Start to see your life as the most
Incredible ride,
START
Taking a few moments out to
STOP
Breathe
And
LISTEN
Just some of advice to put the torment in remission

THE REAPER IS COMING

I don't want to break this to you

But

One day

You won't be around

Ohhhhhhh
It's no easy to hear is it?
One day you could end up on the other side of the ground

The reaper is coming and you can't keep running

It's up to you what you do
When you hear that

97

You could take a step back
Have a look what's going on
Or
Keep your head down
Stumbling on,
Till one day eventually
Your time has come,
To be completely honest
I can't tell you EXACTLY
What awaits for us on the other side,
And if someone has told you EXACTLY what happens
I'm afraid they've lied,
I do have my own ideas
But it wouldn't be fair to mislead,
The truth is
You don't know what's going to happen tomorrow
Life's a crazy ride and nothing's guaranteed,

But

The reaper is coming and you can't keep running

I'm not trying to scare you like MJ's Thriller,
I'm just stating the truth
The truth can be killer,
But dying is easy
It's living that's the hard part
When you don't fear death that's when you can start,
To truly smile,
Because the thought of death can inspire great things
And makes life worthwhile,
You have a very short time to make your own individual impact
This is a pretty significant fact,
Because

The reaper is coming and you can't keep running

This powerful knowledge puts everything into perspective,
Grab life by the horns
You'll be more effective,
Is that 60 hour working week honestly worth it?
If you're just going to sit and complain,
Don't you have a compelling feeling for a bigger purpose?
A higher aim,
It's fine if you truly enjoy what you do
But not many do,
And that is just true,
Is that pent up worry and anger really what you need,
Or is it time to accept and concede,

That

The reaper is coming and you can't keep running

The fear of death
Stems from
The fear of life

Those who fully live will be prepared for their fate,
Start living NOW
Don't leave it too late,

Take great risks
Be prepared to fail
Spend time looking after the old, weak and frail,
Take a lesson away every time you feel you lose
There's a lot to be learnt every time you bruise,
Take responsibility for every move you make
It's ok!
Everybody's made a mistake,

You have to accept sometimes you can't have everything you desire
It sparks your passion it sparks your fire,
Don't let a petty argument destroy a great friend
When you think about it
Is it really worth it in the end?
When it comes to change greet it with open arms
It never has to be time to signal the alarms,
COME ON
GET UP
Explore places you've never been
It doesn't have to be a fantasy or a dream,
Design your ideal life
Let your imagination run wild
Never ever lose your sweet inner child,
Yes
The reaper may be coming and there's nowhere to hide
But when you begin to live life by the fullest
My friends
You go down with your pride.

MUNDANE MONDAY (PART 4)

He wakes up to the sound of
beeeeeeep beeeeeep beeeeep
And he knows it's time to start his chore,
When he sleeps it's the only time he rests
Because in his head it's a constant war,
He's been trashed out his mind
Friday Saturday Sunday
It's Monday
So he's ready to break,
His eyes might be open but his mind's fully shut
Inside he's never awake,
So he sparks up a spliff to lift him out of bed,
As he turns on the T.V. the weather man said,
"Heavy showers today"
"Possible thunder"

"And dark"
"Dark skies"
So he heads to the bathroom and he rolls his eyes,
The warm water from the shower momentarily washes away the dull
pain,
But he quickly realises he's going to be late for work
So he misses breakfast
And heads to the rain,
The thunder and lightning crashes down,
craaaaaaash craaaaaaaash crassssssh
So he picks up his pace and pedals faster,
Turning up late for work again could end up a total disaster,
A lorry flies past,
hoooooonk hooooooonk
Soaking him through to the bone,
Head's screaming should have stayed at home
But even there he's all alone
He stops riding for a minute as he answers the phone,
du du dudu du du dudu du du du dududuu

"hello"

"oi!"
"You little prick"
"Make sure you get me that 100 quid by the end of the day"

(He's in massive debt after the weekend from some banging MDMA)

"errrrm mate"
"I'm struggling here"
"My rent's due"
"I swear I'll get it you by the end of the week,"

"Get it to me by Friday or I'm going to Fucking freak,"

He arrives to work 15 minutes late
His boss is there waiting,
"This really is your final chance now lad"
"Please don't bother debating",
He heads upstairs
Sits on his chair
Looks aimlessly at a computer screen,
Wondering how he went from man
To pilot mode machine,

All day he's surrounded by fingers tapping
click click click click

Phones singing
riiing riing   riiing riiing

People
chattering   chattering
chattering   chattering

He's getting a slight migraine now
Because his ears have had a constant battering,

Sarah who's sat across chirps over
"So,"
"You know Dan right?"

"No,"

"Well he's going out with Molly-May",

He tries his hardest to listen in
To hear what she has to say,
But just hears

"blaaah blaaah blaaaah"
"Kissing"
"Blaaaah blaaah blaaah blaaah"
"Sex"
"Blaaaah blaaah blaaah blaaah"
"Cheating"
Blaaaah blaaah blaaah blaaah
"Fighting"
Blaaaah blaaah blaaah blaaah
"Crying"
Blaaaah blaaah blaaah blaaah
"SLAG"
Blaaaah blaaah blaaah blaaah
"SLUT"
Blaaaah blaaah blaaah blaaah

"SARAH!"
"Please shut up"

He grins and bears the rest of work
But he's aching to get back and get high,
This isn't the way he envisioned his life
Part of a rat race   waiting to die,

The end of his shift finally comes,
He shoots straight to Ladbrokes where he knows his luck's about to come in,
He's got to make some money back after the weekend so after a big BIG win,
1 hour later
He's another 100 quid down the drain
He heads outside and he's back in the rain,
He's completely clueless
He throws down his guard,

It's gone way past anger now
And rage hits him hard,
He finds the nearest shop
Grabs a bottle of jack,
Makes his way to the local train station
There ain't no turning back,
On his way there he can't understand how his life turned out like this,
Dreams and ambitions have been lost in the total abyss
At one stage he had girls queuing up for a kiss
Now he just feels like a useless soul
That nobody   would miss,
A few moments away from his 'get off''
He bumps into his old best mate Steve,
The angels were looking out for him that day
Because what happens next
You wouldn't believe

They sat down together
He could no longer fight back his tears,
Steve held him tight
Said
"It'll be alright"
"Don't worry"
"Sack your fears,"
"This is just a part of your life"
"We can overcome NOW together,"
"Time to learn to ride the waves during turbulent weather,"
"I was talking about you the other day"
"We discussed how much we miss you,"
"There are so many people that adore you"
"I just wish you"
"Could see"
"If you weren't around man"
"It would totally break me,"

"Whether it be"
"Poor self-esteem   chronic stress   grief   financial stability"
"It's nothing we can't get past"
"I promise you bro 100%"
"This pain will not last,"
"You've really got to feel the wet to experience the glisten,"
"But from heart to heart"
"To man to man"
"I have some true advice so please just listen,"

Steve grabs the bottle of jack
Throws it away,
Looks his broken friend in the eyes
Doesn't hold back what he has to say,

"Finding answers at the end of a bottle,"
"What'll,"
"That really do for you?"
"If happiness is what you wish to pursue"
"I think it's the time of the start of something new,"
"I mean Mandy"
"Might be handy"
"For getting randy"
"Intimate close and deep"
"But remember how you feel with no serotonin dopamine and sleep,,"
"The amount of times I've seen you heaped up weeping mess upon the floor"
"But for some reason"
"This shit"
"You chose to ignore,,"
"Are suicide Mondays really worth it?"
"Is the juice worth the squeeze?"
"Use your head"
"Be smart my friend"

"Stop falling on your knees,,
"It's a joke,"
"How much coke"
"You can actually get through in one night,"
"No wonder you're a broken man"
"You've lost vision and your sight,"
"I mean"
"I remember back in my high days"
"Thought that I could fly days"
"Never wondered why days"
"Part of a hazy maze"
"Looking for a place to blaze"
"Fitting into part of a craze"
"But know I'm on my next phase"
"If you're this unhappy man"
"It's time for you change your ways,"
"I ain't trying to talk to you like FRANK"
"And say all drugs are bad Mckay,,
"I'm just saying there's other shit you can do on your day to day,"
"In no way at all am I saying"
"JUST SAY NO,"
"BUT if it's impeding on your health"
"Something got to go bro,"
"Remember how talented you are!"
"You gave up on your music, creativity and art,"
"You let your mind take over"
"You stopped living with your heart,"
"The days I've seen you happiest"
"Is when we have a 90 minute game of football"
"Go to the gym"
"Followed by a run,"
"No wonder you're a broken man when you sit slobbing like a bum,"
"Think back to when we'd be around yours"
"We'd laugh straight"

"Easily for an hour,"
"You're the only one that can change this round man"
"It's you who has the power,"
"Remember"
"Hardship prepares an ordinary person"
"For an extraordinary fate,"
"There's enlightenment round the corner man"
"It's well worth the wait,"
"There's a reason we crossed paths today"
"It could have been fate or it could have just been by chance,"
"But the only way I can help you make sense of change is"
"Plunge into it"
"Move with it"
"Join in with the dance"

YOU'VE GOT THIS

I can see your pain and I can see your confusion,
But don't let
That's it
Game over
Life's done
Become your conclusion,
Because
YOU'VE GOT THIS

The whirlwind that you're in is the beginning
Of something wonderfully new for you,
So let's start to look life through
The wisdom
Hurt
Sorrow in our heart,

Be smart,
Rejoice now
How you wanna act is a choice now,
So
Take the

Right step

But

That's left

To you

You can look down
But that's
Up
To you,
There's no secret magic spell or voodoo
That can show you,
YOU'VE GOT THIS
So stop this,
Holding on to hot coal
It'll rot your soul,
You can
Look in every book in every library shelf
That'll try and stabilise your mental health,
But you know
You're the only one with the trigger
And that's for you to figure out
So don't doubt it
Stand up and shout it
IV'E GOT THIS

Remind yourself this everyday
Let it guide the way
'every little thing's gonna be ok'
Today is a new day

REMEMBER
It comes
It goes
What's best?
Who knows?
Just treat yourself like the cold wind
blows
YOU'VE GOT THIS

GOODBYE MANDY

You were my clear crystal mistress
We met that mysterious night,
Bitter in taste
I was told not to bite,
You had me all spaced out
I couldn't resist your adventure,

Buzzing off your chemicals,
Speaking from my head
Not my genitals,

Had me shaking
Lost in mind,
Then you held me gently
Your touch felt kind

New meeting
Heart beating
Nervous I admit,
Lip biting
Exciting
Energy you emit,

The moment you left the party
I never wanted to stay,
I just wanted you back
But there was a big price to pay,
Although our love was strong
It never felt true,
Goodbye Mandy
I'll never forget you

DON'T LOOK BACK

Momentary illusion
Conclusion is yours,
Floors creaking
Freaking you out,
Doubt you'll get back
Lack of light,
Fight to keep strong
Long way to go,
Flow like a ride
Stride in your step

DANGER

DANGER... DANGER...
DANGER...
Should I or shouldn't I?
DANGER... DANGER... DANGER...
Might just give it a try
DANGER... DANGER... DANGER...
Only strangers fill this place
DANGER... DANGER... DANGER...
Can they see this nervous look on my face?
DANGER... DANGER... DANGER...
Everyone else seems to be doing just fine
DANGER... DANGER... DANGER...
But your mum, dad and school told you not to walk down this line,
DANGER... DANGER... DANGER...
How bad could it be?
DANGER... DANGER... DANGER...
Ingrained inside of me.

BREATHE

breathe *breathe* *breathe*

There's beauty in all moments of life
You can find it within the breath,
I wrote this poem the day after the crash
Felt compelled to tell what I learnt
The day I cheated
Death

breathe

"Singing don't worry about a thing"
"Because every little thing"
"It's gonna be alright"
"Rise up this morning smiled with the rising sun"
"3 little birds pitch by my door step"

"Singing sweet songs of melodies pure and true"
"Saying this is my message to"

car horn
Huuuuuuuuu huuuuuuuu
CRASH
BANG
CRAAASH
fast breathing

"SHIT"
"What the flipping hell's happening"
I'm on my back
There's a car on its way
I close my eyes
Clench my fists
Accept this is it…
I die today

Five seconds later

I slowly open my eyes
To my surprise

I'M ALIVE!

BREATHE

Scramble around shattered glass
Quickly recover my cap,
Kick the door with all my force
Squeeze through the tightest gap,
Stand up tall
Look around
Presented by three businessmen,

"Are you alright mate?"
"WHAT THE FUCK HAPPENED?"
They query again
Again and again,

I look puzzled
To be honest
I didn't actually have a clue,
First I was driving
Then I was surviving,
"If this is heaven I didn't expect the angels to look like you"

One sits me down shouts
"CALM DOWN"
"DON'T WORRY"
"THERE'S A CHANCE YOU'LL GO INTO SHOCK"
"What's your name?"
"Where you from?"
"What speed were you doing on the clock?"

BREATHE

Exchange looks at those around
See mouths moving
But can't hear a sound,
Get a flash back of being air bound
As I slowly gaze my vision back down to the ground,

neeeeeeeenoooor
neeeeeeeeeeeenoooor
neeeeeeeeeenoooor

Ambulance and police arrive on the scene
Get the cones out like a football team,
Traffic starts flowing in steady stream

Police man says
"Nice parking mate"
"Bit extreme"

Summoned to the back of a bright yellow van
Poked and prodded by the paramedic man,
While being questioned like the weakest link
"Hello Anne"

BREATHE

When I arrived home
My mind began to roam,
Sat in a silent stillness I've never really felt
With a scent in the air I've never really smelt,
Taste of blood in my mouth as I'd been touching the cut on my
knee,
Looking aimlessly at the vivid bright colours beaming back at me,

The shoulda coulda wouldas
Began to carousel,

Could this be heaven or could it be hell?

BREATHE

Hunched over the kitchen table
Head in hands
Mind begging to crack,
My dad stood beside me
And placed his hand on my back,
Took a deep breath
Words started to exchange
"In one split second life can change"
"That doesn't sink in until in a split second life does actually

change"
"Today my friend you survived the firing range"
"It can take an event like this to realise how much you have"
"Keep that inside implanted"
"There's so much that surrounds us we always take for granted"
"You may have limitations
But how you spend your time is always a choice"
"Always believe in yourself
Trust your inner voice,"
"Every morning you wake up in a warm cosy bed"
"Every night you have a place to rest your tired weary head,",
"There's no hurricane, tornado or natural disaster outside your
door"
"You live in a safe place that isn't riddled with constant war"
"Access to food you like"
"A roof that isn't leaking"
"People who care for you and will always listen when you're
speaking"

We are born in one day
We die in one day,
Anything can happen
In just one day,
So
Love when you can
Love while you can
Love as much as you can

You've rocked the boat now
It's time to sail smart,
Forgive often
Smile with all your heart,
DON'T
Hold off life and wait patiently in the queue,

Because one single moment can obliterate everything you ever knew,

Never forget the moment you stared back at the reaper
And waved away death,
Because you'll remember to find beauty
In
Every
Single
Breath

THE LITTLE BOOK

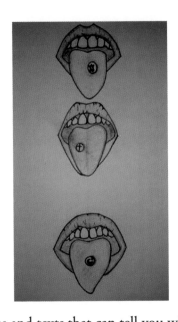

There are scriptures and texts that can tell you what's best,
A book to help guide you if you practice its values,
When you have done bad you can redo your wrong,
By twisting your tongue,
Sin then start from the beginning,
The book prevents you from going astray,
Or losing your way,
It captures the hateful and turns them to pray,
Some know the words word for word,
Speak, recite the words some seem to find their own meaning,
Do we need to read to learn how to be?
Or is there goodness ingrained in you and me?
Are these writings binding us or blinding us,
My religion simply is kindness,

It's wise to be simple and simply kind,
That's the religion that eases my mind,

The creator of the book made me not believe in him,
But believing in anything other than him is to sin,
So should I be punished for not believing in he?
I tend to only believe what I see,
If he is all light and almighty,
Will he still have the faith in me?
Teachings tell me not to rape, cheat or murder but that's not
something I've ever thought to do,
I've heard stories of rape, cheat and murder from people who take
these writings as true,
Do a set of rules guide you right,
Or do you find your own way in what feels alright,
Are you the strength when learning to stand?
Or do you ask the sky for a helping hand?

It's wise to be simple and simply kind,
That's the religion that eases my mind,

They tell me to love thy neighbour,
Unless he is gay apparently some say,
There's a ban on a man liking another man,
But can you force how you feel?
Or is it part of his master plan,
There's love and lust in all of us,
Maybe the lords a little bi curious,
If he demands hate on those who are in love,
I don't want to be invited when I die
To the sky above.

TRIBUTE POEM

As I took centre stage,
I looked down,
And
Suddenly
It all made sense to me,
Everything written on the page fits together,
Making a perfect shape,
I couldn't believe
I had written this,
Masterpiece,
I had formed these words,
Assembled such a jigsaw,
With vision,
Wisdom,
And honesty,
Honestly,
This had all come from me,

The audience,
Laughed,
Winced,
Sighed,
Cried,
Then roars of applause,
To follow,
I get flashbacks
Of the clicks, snaps,
And claps,
Those in the room
Who had lost their path,
Found a lantern,
I somehow found a way,
To articulately say,
My anger towards the world's politics,
Without losing my mind
Or point,
Those who just needed a smile,
Smiled brighter,
Than the flowers,
I spoke about in the poem,
It had flow,
With reason,
Like the changing of the seasons,
It knew when
And where
To
STOP.

And
Then
I woke.
This is not the poem
This is
Just a tribute.

ANIMAL BEHAVIOUR

I've lived and grown up on a farm,
Now
You can imagine at school the harm that could cause,
Of course kids will find something to scrutinise you with,
"Barn boy", "sheep shagger", "Mr. manure" was a particular favourite
of mine,
I'll let you figure out the rest,

I didn't mind,
In fact this was the best I could have asked for seeing as I was also
fat…,
It wasn't long until they held that against me too,
When that was used towards me it was a little more raw,
And when they saw how sore that hurt they used it more.
But I never let bullies and low life losers get the better of me,

Actually… quite the opposite,
I let it… drive me,
I let it… push me, through the tightest of gaps,
You couldn't shush me or keep me silent even on the darkest of paths.
But it did lead me to spend a lot more time at home undisturbed on
the farm,
I had more common ground there,
I liked the calm surroundings and lack of aggression,
Family and friends liked to tell me I'm lonely, suffering depression,
But never asked the question, "Why is it you spend time on your own?"
My answer would have been,
"I'm never alone,"
You see people were not my go-to,
I'd grow to stay away from the confusion they'd learnt to understand,
I couldn't unravel the reason they found it so easy to hurt one another,
I didn't feel I was taking cover or living in the gutter,
I just found it easy to not get caught up in it all,
Like a mouse getting caught up in a trap for the smallest amount of
cheese,
Knowing full well the juice wasn't worth the squeeze,
But still pursuing it because… well… why not?
So I decided to not…,
But with that I got to spend most of my time with animals,
There was a simplicity and charm in them I recognised,
I didn't feel they had anything to disguise or hide,
And likewise,
I felt absolutely free and accepted in me,
The thing that I really appreciated - they weren't afraid to appear
exactly how they felt.
If they were scared they'd be scared,
If they were angry they'd let you know,
If they wanted affection they'd show you love,
I didn't realise how important this could be for me as I grew older,
I wasn't just going to put on a front and wear a face because I was told to,

"That's just what people do,"
I wanted to stay true, loyal, remain authentic to the moment,
I carried out this animal instinct attitude towards my writing.
When I feel attacked I'll write with the ferocity of a dog that's been backed into a corner,
I'll be faithful and protective when my voice is not heard,
I'll write with playfulness and exuberance as if a ball's just been hurled in the air,
I'll have the tenderness and care in my words when love feels lost,
I'll be friendly, intelligent and quiet if I feel that's what the world needs,
Never be scared to show exactly where you're at,
Never be afraid to act how the now tells you to,
Be strong, use your sense, don't get manipulated,
Let your inner animal guide you,
Let your inner animal carry out the pride inside of you.

LEAVE WITH LOVE

*Love is all I came with
And love is all I'll leave behind,
Everything else is temporary
And for that
I don't mind*

*When I leave
I'll leave with love,
And for me
That's enough,
I have a bank full of memories
Which have left me feeling spent,
Good times can come at quite a cost
And it was worth every cent,
My time is my only penny,
I'm counting my moments*

Making my moments count
Amount of money
Was once the object
Amount of objects
Was once the aim,
I can make the claim
That I've played that game
And it all felt the same,

We're here now on borrowed time,
My zone feels still
While I'm dealing with the hand I'm dealt,
Tick to tock to tock to tick
Life changes in a
click
The clock only looks forward
So am I facing the right way then?
Stand big like Ben
While counting back from
10...9...8...7...6...5
I couldn't feel more alive,
It's time to shine,
The world is beautiful
As you are bright
Enjoy the light
Find acceptance in the night,
The rain will fall
But the sun shall glow
This is how flowers grow,
Remember though
The most colourful flowers will one day get old
And someday will wilt
Always remember what love built,

Foundations of friends holding strong
With laughter that cements together,
The weather has tested
The structure protected
The roof remains strong up above,

Love is all I came with
And love is all I'll leave behind,
Everything else is temporary
And for that
I don't mind

LIFE'S BEAUTIFUL GAME (PART 5)

"Dad Dad Dad!"
"Come on get up it's time to go to the park"

"Ahhhhhhh come on mate"
"Get in bed a sec"
"It still looks pretty dark,"
"But Dad"
"DAD!"
"You said we could go early in the morning"
"Dad starts yawning,"
"In bed now or the tickle monster's coming out and that's the final warning,"
Mum speaks up
"Go on you said you would and anyway more bed for me"
"Before you go flick us on the kettle bring us up a cuppa tea,"

So it's 7am
And for some reason Charlie and his dad have ended up on the park
Both kitted up doing kicky ups,
Now
These 2 are football mad
They'd get their boots on any opportunity they had,
See
Dad's always had
A competitive side
He really tried to tone it down,
But if Charlie'd score he'd score 2 more,
He wasn't afraid to go in there with a bit of a shoulder
But he said "it'll give you strength when you're growing older,"
He liked to relate life lessons to football
He'd say
"Son"
"No matter how big, small or tall you are
You don't stop and cry when you hit the bar",
"Sometimes in life things don't go our way"
"But you've gotta keep playing the game even on a windy day,"
As his dad is talking
Charlie hits the ball sweet with his left like you wouldn't believe!
His dad looks back in amazement and says
"WOW"
"Now that's our cueto leave",

5 years on where has the time gone

Charlie's getting ready for his first day at high school,
Smart shirt, blazer on, black tie
Cool…
He heads down stairs smelling like he's used more men's cologne,
Than Superdrug own,
Shouts "Mum I'm leaving"

But she's on the phone,
As he gets in the kitchen he sees an orange shoe box on the table with a
swoosh tick on the side with a note on the top saying
'Wear them with pride,'
As he opens the box
He reveals the most beautiful black and white football boots you ever
have seen
He wonders if he's really awake or if he's still in a dream,
Inside the left boot he found a small folded letter
It started with
'From dad try these maybe they'll fit you better,'
It went on to say
'Listen son
I couldn't be more proud of you,
You put 110% effort in everything that you do,
You're polite and friendly to every single person you meet,
You're honest and caring and I know you don't cheat,
Seriously man
Good luck today I know you'll do alright,
But remember the first rule my boy
Always shoot on sight,'

As Charlie read that he had a smile on his face
Heading out the door laughing with a tear to his eye,
If he could move any quicker
He would touch the sky,

5 years on where has the time gone

It's Charlie's cup final!
His whole family have gone to watch the game,
They couldn't believe the amount of people there screaming his name,
As the starting whistle blows
He looks over to his dad

Who's standing on the side line
Trying to look fine
Holding up a big sign,
But he can see the nerves in his eyes and the tension in his hands
But Charlie's got a job to do as he waves to his fans,
Half time whistle comes and they're 1-0 down,
As Charlie heads off to the changing rooms he's wearing a frown,
But his dad grabs his arm before he wanders out of sight,
He said
"Remember what I said about the bar son
You don't cry you always fight,"

20 minutes into the second half,

Dan picks the ball up on the by line,
Dan over to Alfie
Alfie through to Steve,
Steve takes 4 men on (he's got a lot of tricks up his sleeve),
Steve back to Dan,
Who turns past his man,
Lofts it over to Chris
Chris darts down the right
The goal is now in sight,
Plays a one two with Andy
Ball whipped in,
Body flies in,
And
BIG HEAD BY TOM,
GOAL!
1-1
The game is truly on,
The final whistle approaching and Charlie receives the ball from Steve,
Takes a touch
Has a look up…

He hits a shot sweet with his left like you wouldn't believe!
It goes completely silent
…
As it glides in the roof of the net,
The crowd start roaring losing their minds this is a moment he'll never forget,
Game over
2-1
The final whistle's been blown,
The crowd were making noises completely unknown,
The first move Charlie makes he shoots over to his dad,
He hugs him
They laugh
His dad gives him 50 quid and says
"Have a good night you've earned it me lad,"

5 years on where has the time gone

We're in the hospital now and Charlie has a baby on the way,
Let's just say he can really shoot
I'm not just talking about his football boot,
Both families are in the waiting room it's silent and still the cat has everyone's tongue,
As Charlie and his girlfriend are in the labour ward and she's screaming out her lungs,
2 hours on
And finally
They're presented with their new delicate baby boy,
Charlie holds him in his arms and sobs with tears of love and joy,
As he gets out the ward door
In the corridor,
He is welcomed by his dad,
He just takes a look up and says
"you alright granddad"

They fall in each other's arms and hold each other tight
His dad says
"I told you son I said you'd do alright,"
This isn't going to be easy you know they'll be days where it's like
drawing Barcelona away
"Come on dad"
"I've got my boots tied up"
"I've learnt from the best"
"I'm ready to play"

5 years on where has the time gone

Charlie his dad and little max are now together playing in the park,
They've been kicking about for ages now and it's getting pretty dark,
Max picks up the ball and places it sturdy on the spot,
Takes about 20 steps back
Eyes it up
And gets ready to take the shot,
Charlie and his dad look back at him
Smile and grin,
Both shout
"THIS ONE FOR THE WIN"
Max runs up
Hits a shot sweet with his left like you wouldn't believe,
Charlie and his dad both look back in amazement and say
"WOW"
"Now that's our cue to leave,"
On the drive back they're all singing
"Football's coming home it's coming home it's coming"
As Charlie's on the dash board drumming,
As his dad looks around he says

"Cherish these moments because life's about the memories you make,,
As he pulls up to the house he puts his foot on the brake,

He says
"Sometimes in life you need to be more like a goalkeeper take a back
seat and just observe the game,"
"Some people in life take their eye off the ball miss the most
magnificent moments"
"And that's a true shame,"
Charlie looks back at his dad and says
"You know what"
"You're not too bad for an old lad,"
Max waves his granddad goodbye
They both look at each other with love in their eye,

5 years on where has the time gone

We're in the hospital again
And this time it isn't great news,
Granddad's not got long left
the final whistle's approaching and we've surrendered to lose,
The whole family are gathered around the side of the bed,
Charlie's holding his hand as he slowly turns his head,
He said,
"Son"
"Look after the girls and my little man Max",
"I know they'll be alright and you'll keep him on the right tracks,"
"Remember what I told you about living for today,"
"To find peace is in the moment and there ain't no other way"
"You can't always just look at the goal you need to focus on the steps
leading there"
"Concentrate on every moment with precision and care,"
"I'll never forget the first time I saw you hit the ball sweet with your
left like I couldn't believe,"
"My time's coming up son but it isn't time to grieve,"
"Just remember the beautiful memories we had and times spent up on
the park,"

"When we'd kick the ball for hours and hours get lost within the dark,"

2 hours on

Granddad's passed away
We're at the final part of the story now it's the morning of the next day,

Charlie and Max are around granddad's, cleaning around the house

As Charlie goes in his old bedroom
He sees an orange shoe box with a Nike swoosh tick laid upon the bed,
As he opens it
He finds a small folded letter
He smiles and he shakes his head,
It read,
'Boys this one's for you,'
'Now this isn't time to cry,'
'Everyone's going to die,'
'It's time to remember the days we were all flying high,'
'So here's some advice I thought I'd put it in standard formation,'
'Through ways you're going to understand it
'Through football translation,'
'MAXY'
'When it comes to girls don't just go route one'
'Have tactics   play it simple   and take your time,'
'Trust me the right one will come along it'll damn sure be worth the climb,'
'Sometimes the one with the highest power like the referee'
'Is going to be a dick,'
'You can't just get angry and scream son'
'Play it smart or it'll make you sick,'
'There's a reason why Messi and Ronaldo have worked their way to the top,'
'That's through'
'Passion   dedication   and training non-stop,'

'Learn from the best players'
'They look up   have composure   always work on their self-control,'
'If you make a mistake put your hands up'
''s important for your soul,'
'CHARLIE'
'When you're arguing with Sarah'
'You have to remember why she became your lover companion and your best friend,'
'Go out there and treat her it doesn't have to be football every weekend,'
'LADS'
'Take every opportunity there are so many wonderful things you can do,'
'Aim and shoot for the stars my boys'
'I'm so proud of you two.'

MY FAMILY

Here's a thank you,
For the wise words and actions shown to me,
Set me free,
Gave me vision,
Helped me see,
Open mind,
Let me be,

****************MUM****************
You've displayed what the mind can conceive,
Start to believe,
Anything at all is possible to achieve,
And that's why we've… grown stronger,
Because I've learnt to no longer,
Let my mind hold me back,

Start to create the right track,
No man is an island
But always watch your back,
You inspire to inspire,
Determination, drive I admire,
Always reminded me there's no smoke without a fire,
You said
"Strive not to be a success"
"But rather be of value",
That's how you'll,
Keep a happy mind,
It's easier to be kind,
you'll find,
Something I remember you embodied when I was young and small,
You must make a choice to take a chance or your life will never change at all,
You said, "Life is 10% what happens to you 90% of how you react,"
"Get up off your arse"
"STOP MOANING"
"It's not getting you anywhere and that is a fact,
I know at times we've kept our distance,
But without your help and assistance,
I would never have discovered the most difficult thing in life is the decision to act … the rest is merely tenacity and persistence,

*****************NOW DAD*****************
Your teaching has differed… but you balanced me right out,
I learnt not every time you get in a debate
Do you need to scream and shout,
I see from you
Life isn't about getting and having
It's all about giving and being,
It's the one way to find solace in your own mental well-being,

142

A person who never made a mistake
Never tried anything new,
A man is a success if he gets up in the morning
Goes to bed at night
In between does what he wants to do,
Don't worry about money you can't buy back time,
Remember the better the view at the top
The harder and higher the climb,
You said,
"Just start where you are"
"Use what you have"
"Do what you can",
'BIG LOVE' for your constant wisdom and honesty man,
You told me the real secret to life is to completely engage with the
here and now
Instead of calling it work
Realise it's play,
I can't wait for the moment I have a son or daughter and tell them
this someday.

****************BIG SIS******************
Well well well
We didn't get off to a great start,
But the older we grew,
The more I knew,
You always had a lion sized heart,
You've shown me
You can't fall if you don't climb
But there's no joy in living your life on the ground,
Opportunities come
Opportunities go
But they always come back around,
You may be disappointed if you fail
but you're doomed if you don't try,

It's seeing you constantly better yourself that makes me want to fly
high,
I remember looking at you and thinking
If all you do is talk
You are just repeating the things you already know,
If you learn to be a silent observer
It's the time you build and grow,
You were the wisest one in making our house a happy home,
Because when I couldn't help but wind you up
You taught me muddy water is best cleared by leaving it alone,

NOW...
We've all had our tricky days
But our love just grew and grew,
Found the best way out
Is always through,
Tough times never last
But tough people do,
I couldn't be more proud and honoured to learn from every single
one of you.
*********************x*******************

6 WAYS TO CALM THE STORM AND BEGIN TO SEE

Are you lost?

Your vision is hazy and the storm won't let you see,
No idea where you are?
Where you're going?
Or where you want to be?

You're forever looking for that fairy tale land,
No anxiety
No depression
Just Crystal Ocean and golden sand,
Well

You're never too far adrift
You can always find your way back to shore,
The more you truly believe in yourself

Your feet will soon touch the floor,
If you really want to dampen the storm
And find your missing part,
It's time to stop thinking with the mind
And start feeling
With the heart,

Whatever you've experienced in life has been carved into stone

But

Let every event create a good you,
Learn from your mistakes
They'll improve you view,

You have the power to change the way you feel right now,
Be brave
Shim far beyond shallow waters
Plunge deep for the peal in existence,
Know you can go the distance,
If people are constantly hurting you
There are wounds that still need healing,
Start to search inside yourself
Some truths will be revealing,
So
Here are some possible reasons you may be feeling lost deep inside,
Try and listen in
It may help you calm the ride,

1) Stop letting people walk all over you! Have your own viewpoints stand tall and be strong, Just because others have different opinions doesn't   mean they're right and you're wrong
2) You don't love yourself! You barely even like yourself! Each morning when you wake up you have the ability to love or

hate who you are, be careful which you chose, one you'll go far and the other will scar

3) There is a passion and a purpose you are still yet to discover, you will never find it if you only take cover

4) Don't look to others for comfort and answers only you can provide, see the world through your own lens and trust yourself as a guide

5) Spend more time in nature the place where we truly belong, the more time you spend in the great outdoors you'll be back to feeling strong

6) You can't keep surrounding yourself with people who make you feel uninspired, it's time to get assertive let them go, and tell them straight 'you're fired'

4.5 BILLION YEARS

The world is around 4.5 billion years old,
So we're a blip in a timeline of a story we're told,
All those problems
Feelings
Hurting inside,
Don't take life too seriously because you're part of a ride,
There are ups
There are downs
It's over so fast,
So don't spend your time getting stuck in the past,
Don't just look forward
Worrying
Wondering what's ahead,
Live in this moment
With happiness
Instead

148